Little Pock
Red Flags

A guide to dating in the age of
social media & managing toxic
relationships

By
Louise Pullen
& Shelly Palmer

This Book is a passion project written by
two best friends to empower and educate
women.

From mother to sister to niece to friend. Knowledge is power.
Never settle for anything less than you deserve.
We all rise together

Louise and Shelly x

Acknowledgements

We would like to thank all of those who helped with and worked on this project.

Adman Lawman
Graham Torr
Helen Martin
Malory Torr
David Palmer
Alan Clews

We would also those who supported and championed this project from the start you know who you are.

Aka our Royal Family.

About the Authors

Louise and Shelly met at Borough sports day when they were twelve years old. They went to two different local schools which were both competing in the competition. After the event, Louise invited Shelly to the roller disco with her friends. And as they say, the rest is history.

Well, not quite. There are lots of stories in between, but we can save those for another time.

They are two South London girls that have grown up together. They have been in each other's lives throughout three decades.

They have shared laughter joy and heart break side by side. They have shared the feelings of a breakdown of a relationship, their first girl's holiday and double dated with their first boyfriends together. There is not much Shelly and Louise have not done together.

And, more importantly, they have both had to rebuild their lives after experiencing toxic relationships with controlling partners. With this book they want to empower women to take back the power that was taken from them.

They have also discovered that throughout both their journeys they actually have voices and something to say. Voices that were lost for a short while. These are two strong independent women with a story to tell. They hope their story will reach and inspire others to recognise that they have a voice too.

They want to educate those who have lost their voice due to toxic people, so that they can spot the signs and ensure that they do not get involved and entwined with these people ever again.

Although their lives are different and they have taken different paths, their friendship has remained the same through all these years. They have been each other's strength and support during the highs and lows which only life can throw at you.

Their friendship has endured the test of time. And I think it is safe to say I think they will be friends for life.

Knowledge is power and this book will help you to recognise the danger signs, when to hear those alarm bells and take action. Take back the power. Regain your voice.

Louise Pullen

Louise has three dependent children, two of which have additional needs. Louise was in a toxic relationship for fifteen years.

Dr. Lillian Glass, a California-based psychology expert who is seen as coining the term in her 1995 book *Toxic People*, defines a toxic relationship as "any relationship [between people who] don't support each other, where there's conflict and one seeks to undermine the other, where there's competition, where there's disrespect and a lack of cohesiveness." Toxic relationships can be mentally, emotionally and sometimes physically damaging to one or both participants.

Having had the strength to leave this toxic relationship, Louise bravely stepped back out into the world of dating after fifteen years. Feeling like Bambi on ice, she tentatively dipped her toe into a world which had changed from the one she had once remembered. This new world was driven by social media and was full of snap chats, memes and the risk of women receiving the occasional dick pic.

The image of Bambi soon turned into a scene reminiscent of Jaws, hence how you come to be reading this pocket book of Red Flags.

As both Shelly and Louise have wasted a large part of their lives dating men which they should have avoided, looking back they wished they had the tools and the knowledge that they do now.

They have both seen family members and friends go through similar experiences. They could see history repeating itself and they felt that a book like this was desperately needed.

Hindsight can be tough. They wish they had had this guide for their younger selves.

Shelly Palmer

Shelly spent a long time in a relationship with a man who mentally controlled her. He told her how to dress and at times was abusive. Like Louise, Shelly came out of a long-term relationship and stepped back into the world of modern dating.

In that time of sampling dating apps, social media and real life, Shelly found herself dating a married man for six months without knowing the truth about his relationship status. She also dated a man who had her followed by a private investigator after the relationship ended and also dated men, in retrospect she should have only said hello to.

Shelly has described dating post thirty to be like shopping in 'T K Maxx'. You find that designer outfit on the floor only to further discover that the stitches have come undone and the logo has fallen off. Or like buying a second-hand car only to find after driving it for two months that the clutch is faulty, or the breaks fail, and the car catches fire.

After a miscarriage and stepping out with two men

that she should have crossed the road to avoid, Shelly had to rebuild her life into the Queen that she is today. She wants to share her experiences with other women, so that they are aware of how to avoid these types of toxic people.

Shelly and Louise want to help equip women so that they have the tools to recognise these traits and not go through the lessons that these two best friends have had to endure in their lives.

Ladies this book is for you. This is our passion project.

And if it helps one woman, then we will feel that we have achieved all that we set out to do.

However, the goal is for this book –

To be passed from generation to generation – from sister to niece to friend.

To educate women on what is a healthy relationship and what is toxic behaviour.

To understand what toxic behaviour traits are and how to spot them at the onset.

To have a healthy, empowered and happy relationship with yourself and others around you and most importantly, to enable you to leave a relationship when you need to.

Whilst toxic relationships may arise with interaction between friends and family, as well as someone that you are in a relationship with, this pocket book will be focusing on relationships.

In any relationship it is important to have firm healthy boundaries in place. These make a relationship work and last the test of time.

The following can help promote healthy boundaries:

Be clear about your needs.
Be specific and direct.
Be consistent in your verbal communications.
Indulge in healthy banter without getting personal, vindictive or nasty.
Be consistent when it comes to calling and texting.

Maintaining a healthy relationship is keeping the energy consistent. Both parties need to make an effort – a 50/50 effort when it comes to making plans and communicating.

It is important to understand that making an effort in a relationship at any stage of the game is crucial to its success.

For the record we love men. And that has probably been one of our main problems.

We know there are many good men out there. Our mums are married to them. And actually we would like to take a moment to say thank you to our Mums, Angela and Debbie, for all they have done for us. We would also like to apologise for our bad taste in men until recently.

In this book we do not want to label people, we just want to help others become more aware of those toxic people who are out there.

However, the types of people that we are discussing are those with manipulative and toxic behavioural traits. Some of which have genuine personality disorders. Some which might be diagnosable and some which might not be.

Please be aware that these kinds of people can be both men and women.

This book is based on our own personal experiences and those friends who we reached out to, following their own similar personal experiences with these types of people.

We have included their experiences as "Girl Friend Stories" mixed in with our own throughout the book.

Behavioural Traits of Toxic Partners

In our experience toxic partners exhibit certain behavioural traits which can be used to help identify them. Being aware of these traits is your first line of defence against being drawn into a toxic relationship. Many relationships are nowadays formed over social media platforms, so it is no coincidence that this has become the hunting ground of the serial toxic partner. We describe the most common behaviours to be on the lookout for.

<u>Profiling</u>

Men to avoid are the type of men who will message women on social media platforms such as Facebook, Instagram and Snapchat. These men use social media like working professionals use LinkedIn for business. They use social media to stalk women and meet new women at all times, even when they are in relationships. They will study your social media profile and see what type of woman you are.

Have you been through a break-up?
Are you vulnerable?
Are you available emotionally?
What is your financial situation?

Looking at your social media posts such as quotes memes and looking at your interests, your favourite TV shows, hobbies, music and holiday destinations. They will look through your photos if you don't secure your accounts and they will use them to build a mental picture of who you are and what angle they can come at you from.

This is all so that they can figure out what type of person you are. They tend to go for women who they see as having low self-worth and minimal self-esteem. This is because they see such women as being easy to manipulate and lie to.

They can use their lack of confidence against them. They also tend to go for women who have empathic traits who are caring, kind and nurturing.

A friend of ours was dating a guy who admitted that he stalked her on social media before he messaged her and slid into her direct messages.

These men will use the information to their advantage to see if you have any insecurities or where you are vulnerable. This also enables them to become or pretend to become your ideal partner when they met you.

And you'll think when you meet them that they are your dream man, and you'll wonder where they've been all your life. They are like second-hand car salesmen. They'll sell you a dream, but you'll end up buying a nightmare.

Girl Friend Story

A girl friend remembered a conversation that she had with a man on a first date. When he was talking, he would regularly comment on her physical features. Because she did not reciprocate, he began to ask questions about himself to encourage her to complement him.

And she did because she was vulnerable.

He started to drip feed her things about her life which he had seen on her social media.

He made a poignant comment about how he had just given twenty pounds to a homeless person before they met. He failed to mention that this was due to seeing one of her posts about giving money to homeless people.

Having an open Facebook profile enabled this man to view her life and gain an insight into her life. He could see the things she liked and the things she disliked. He could see everything that she wanted her close friends to see. This allowed him to become someone that he thought she would find attractive.

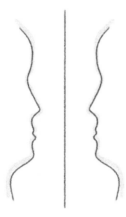

Mirroring

This can come in the form of men pretending to like the same hobbies or interests as you. These men will be watching and waiting for the opportunity to start a conversation with you.

They will even claim that they are interested in the same things or have undertaken the same activities. This gives them the opportunity to slide into your direct messages (DMs).

Never answer these messages. To these types of men you are just a number. To them this is a numbers game. They will send out their DMs and wait like a predator to see who replies. For each of those women they have received just one DM, but these men will be messaging hundreds of women daily. You are not special.

Girl Friend Story – Mirroring

A friend's ex-partner went through all of her Facebook profile before he had met her. He then started a conversation with her based on a Netflix series that her profile had said was in her hobbies and interests section.

It later turned out that the man had never watched the Netflix series at all. He had just used this to start a conversation with her. This, however, was how he gained her trust. This person turned out to be extremely toxic, especially when she found out that he was only using her to make his ex-girlfriend jealous. He had split up with this woman some years ago but he was still unhealthily obsessed with her.

He had told her that he was not in contact with his ex. But when he was presented with his lies, he proceeded to make threats to those who dared tell her the truth. She then had to warn everybody involved and block him from all contact.

Thankfully, he did not carry out his threats. But she later discovered that his ex-girlfriend had to call the police to get a non-molestation order against him when she ended the relationship. This all started from a DM and it shows you just what it can lead to.

They just see you as being available. A suitable target. They are constantly looking for a weakness or an opportunity and your availability on social media can give them exactly what they're looking for.

The Golden Pedestal
(Also known as Love Bombing)

This is the period where they put you high up on a Golden Pedestal and they shower you with complements and attention. Flattery and grand gestures are a common occurrence in this stage.

They will like all of your social media posts and they will message you at all times. They will want and need constant attention including wanting to know where you are and what you are doing.

They will Message you on all platforms such as messenger, text and Instagram throughout any given day. If you prove hard to reach, then they'll try calling several times and even try to make contact through video calls.

Don't be fooled into thinking it's a nice thing when

they start to add your family members and friends on social media. This is just to get close to your network and to get them on side.

You'll see them liking your friends and families posts and offering every ounce of charm.

They'll tag you in memes and quotes and put forward things that you would like such as holiday destinations, films and clothes.

They'll make plans for your future and tell you what you want to hear. It might be a holiday, or it might be children. The fact is it could be anything just to draw you further in.

This is accomplished by using the information that they gather from your social media when they are profiling you right at the very start. They might also ask you questions like what kind of guy you're into, or what your type is. This is to enable them to mould their outward actions to mimic what you have fed them.

It is vital that you do not tell men too much about your past relationships or what your ideal partner is like. This gathering of information will lead them to take you to fancy restaurants or weekends away. Buying you gifts and flowers whilst paying you endless compliments and being attentive to your every need.

You will think that you have died and gone to heaven. You might even ask yourself where this person has been all your life. They will be the ideal partner in every way, and they will slot into your life perfectly. You cannot imagine life before them or without them.

You will feel finally like you're on cloud nine and that you are intoxicated with love. Don't be surprised if the term 'soul mates' comes up early on during this stage as they will want you to believe that you are two peas in a pod or two twin flames that have been separated at birth. They will use the mirroring phase to reinforce this belief.

We have been taken to five-star hotels and taken away on last minute weekends away. We've been sent the early morning texts not long after the late-night texts expressing feelings of undying love. We have sat on the phone for the hour-long conversations where you think that they are genuinely interested in you, but the truth is they're mining for information.

We've been there. We fell for it too. You're not alone. Maybe you just needed someone else to point it out to you. Don't fall for these textbook methods of encapsulating you into their world. The truth is that the Golden Pedestal stage will end. And when it does, that attention and that interest in you as a person will disappear. It may take days, weeks or months. But it will vanish, and you will be left wondering how you got into the situation you are now in.

<u>Gaslighting</u>

How lovely is my white dress?
It's not white. It's black.

A simple example for a dangerous subject. You'll be left feeling dumbstruck that this man will argue against everything you know just to prove that he's right when you know he isn't. He will tell you you're crazy or that there's something wrong with you. He will get personal and vindictive, and he will end up making you question what colour your dress is. And you'll end up wondering if you've gone mad.

You might hear things like 'I'm going out tonight' and it will be the first you've heard of it. But they will tell you that's not true. They will even go into great detail about exactly when they told you and that you just simply don't listen, or you've forgotten.

This could be about spontaneously going out or what you said last Monday. In their mind they are right and you are wrong. You have misheard or you just weren't listening. This is what they will make you think and after long enough, you will sadly begin to believe it.

Even if you catch them lying or cheating, they will still do this. You could have compiled a fifty-page document full of evidence. You could have photographs of them in the act and willing witnesses to give testimonial. Even then they will still tell you that you're wrong. They will tell you that the sky is green just because that's what suits them at the time.

They will shift the blame and twist things around to the point where you will think you are even in the wrong for asking. And there will be a word used many times that you may already be familiar with. Crazy. They will call you crazy and tell you that you need help.

They will be demeaning towards you and put you down. Perhaps you're being oversensitive or it's a certain time of the month. Anything to shift the blame and make you question yourself. They won't give up either, but if they walk away it will be on their terms and that will be the end of the argument, leaving you questioning yourself even more.

Gaslighting is an immensely powerful tool that they use and the more they use it the more you may succumb to it. You start to think that you might be taking things too seriously and that you might be over-thinking things.

You can be gaslighted to the point where you start to

question yourself and you don't know what's right and what's left. You will be emotionally drained, and this is where you will start to give up the fight and let them have their way. You will be exhausted trying to convince them you're not going crazy, but they will not relent, and your confidence and self-assurance will suffer. You will believe your dress is black.

Girl Friend Story – Gaslighting

A man accidentally sent a voicemail to the mother of his children. In it he could be heard discussing with a friend how she was a bad mother. He was moaning that he had to feed their children and that it would cost him a fortune as the mother didn't feed them. He called the children greedy and reiterated that the woman was a bad mother.

However, when the voicemail was shown to him by the mother, he denied that it was him. He even claimed that it was a friend speaking on the phone to which this friend later also stated it wasn't him. When confronted with such clear evidence he denied all knowledge and refuted that it was his voice condemning the mother on the recording. Even though it was clearly him smearing the mother's reputation, when confronted with the evidence the man would not admit nor accept that it was him.

Another Girl Friend Story

A woman was staying round her partner's house one night but the evening developed into an argument. At this stage, the man told the woman that she had to leave as his mother would be round early the next morning. He stated that he had told the woman this information the previous day. The man had got what he wanted and then wanted the woman to leave thus making her feel rejected and weak in comparison to him.

The man had not told her his mother was coming round the day before. This was a lie. He used half-truths to make the story as plausible as he could and to 'wrong foot' the woman. Although the woman knew the man had never told her this, he relentlessly pressed the issue and twisted her mind into believing that he had. The woman left not entirely sure what to believe anymore and the man got his way.

Gaslighting is a powerful tool used to undermine a person's confidence whilst attacking their core beliefs.

Your dress is white. Don't let anyone tell you anything different.

<u>Ghosting</u>

Ghosting is when they have reeled you in via social media but they are not in it for a relationship. They are in it for a quick fix or instant gratification.

Once they get what they want from you, you will probably never hear from them again.

If you try and reach out to them, you will probably find that you have been blocked from every platform going.

You are not alone. They will be doing this with lots of women at the same time.

They are obsessed with the thrill of the chase and the 'honeymoon period'. They want only one thing from you and sadly that is sex. With the sex comes control and dominance over you. You will feel used and they will have got exactly what they wanted.

Some Ghosters may already have a partner or a wife all along. They are on dating sites and chat apps to boost their ego and to make themselves feel attractive. Some might even be open about being in relationships. The point is that when they have obtained what they want from you, it may be sex or it might just be a nude picture, they will ghost you and eradicate your presence from their lives. Watch out for the tell-tale signs of a Ghoster.

Future Faking

This is another form of gaslighting, but it is focused on when someone projects positive thoughts towards the future.

You might hear things like:

In the summer we can book a holiday together.
We should have children.
We should get married.
We should travel the world.
We should buy a house in this area.

Do any of these statements sound familiar? The big difference with these comments is that they will start early on in the relationship and they will come thick and fast. If you have any desires for children, travelling or future plans, they will match them, and they will promise you the world alongside your future with them.

It is a tactic employed to lock you into the relationship early on. They want you to emotionally invest in them and the relationship. Once you have heard all of the amazing promises of things to come, you'll be tied together before you know it.

These things will likely never happen, and they will be repeated over and over again like lines from a well-rehearsed script. Don't think for a second that they haven't been spoken to someone before you and sadly they will likely be said to another woman after you. It is just another form of manipulation employed to entrap you right from the start.

Phasing Out Period

The expression, phasing out, is the same as the saying bait and switch. They bait you in with the love bombing then switch as the mask starts to slide off.

This is also their way of keeping power and control over you. They keep you in a constant state of confusion.

After the dizzying heights of the Golden Pedestal phase you will notice a change in their behaviour. It might happen instantly or over a short period of time. Either way it will be a very confusing and distressing period.

You will find yourself wondering what you did wrong. The texts and phone calls will decrease in frequency and their actions on social media will decline. You might even find that they restrict what you can see or comment on, on their own social media.

You will find that comments are made that slowly chip away at your confidence. They can come in all forms from the way that you dress to the way you walk or carry yourself. Slight digs will begin at how you cook a meal or even wash-up after. You will begin to feel guilty for something you haven't done, and they will increase the volume of negativity to keep you down.

If you ask them about this, they will just say they are busy with work (if they have a job) or that they just need some space. There will be a short excuse for this behaviour, but it will not be justified, and it will not reassure you. The derogatory comments will continue, and they will begin to miss social events or cause an atmosphere if they do turn up. They will berate you in front of others to assert their authority over you.

Now compare this man to the one you first met, the one who couldn't leave you alone and had all the time in the world for you. You have come crashing off the Golden Pedestal from such a great height and you didn't see it coming.

It is common to begin questioning yourself at this stage.

Am I not pretty enough?

Is there another woman?

What did I do wrong?

Did I say something or do something to upset them?

And now we have the reversal of the man's initial role in that you will find yourself texting or calling him more. You might want to find out where he is, who he's with or when he's coming home. You might just want reassurance that everything is ok. What you don't realise is that you are now deep into the game that they've been playing right from the start. The man is secretly enjoying your insecurities and lavishing the attention that you are now placing on him.

Once again this will have a huge impact on your state of mind. Negative and paranoid thoughts will consume you.

Are they bored of me?

What can I do to get them back?

What did I do to make them lose interest?

You will feel crazy as you question yourself and all you will want is the man that you had at the very beginning. The thing is ladies, you never had such a man. It was all just an act. Round after round of one large game to him. Maybe he has a God complex and he feels far superior to every other human being. Maybe he has another woman be her a wife or girlfriend. He might even have kids that you don't know about.

But one thing is true and vital to understand. The man that you met at the beginning was fake. When you go to the cinema or watch a film at home you might find yourself captivated by the performance of certain actors. But you don't for a second believe that their character in the film exists in real life. This should be the same for these men. However, it is our emotional investment and our manipulated minds that stops us from recognising it.

The sad truth is they have got bored of you. The thrill

21

of the chase is over and it is likely that their next victim has caught their eye. Don't be fooled ladies. This is a cruel game to them and they will not understand what it is doing or has done to your head and heart. Pick up on the tell-tale signs. If you can relate to this, then use your experience to never let it happen again.

When It gets Physical

Unfortunately, being involved with a toxic person can lead to physical violence..

Any wrongdoing in the toxic persons eyes could lead to an aggressive or violent response. This could start with them shouting at you for something they think you have done wrong and could quickly escalate into them giving you a shove, slap or worse.

Be warned, if they go in to a rage they can go into full attack mode. They may throw objects, break things and even punch holes in walls or doors. They do this to intimidate you.

If you are brave enough to threaten to leave or to call the police, then try and contact a family member or friend for help.

Please know that they may do anything that they can to stop you from leaving.

They might break down and cry. They might promise to get the help that they need.

This could be rehabilitation or anger management. They will promise gifts, book a romantic weekend away and more.

You could be fooled into thinking they were genuinely remorseful.

Or they might blame you for provoking them in some way. They might go on the defence.

Do not be fooled by any of this behaviour. Their actions will not match their words. And they have no intention of getting the help that they have promised.

Sadly in their warped minds they have done no wrong. You are the one in the wrong.

Even if they are shedding crocodile tears, it is likely that this is a ploy for you to accept their fake apology, and it will happen again and again until you choose to break the cycle.

Horn Dog Hour

Just a brief note on this one. Have you ever been scrolling though Facebook late at night or even in the early hours of the morning? Perhaps it's between one and three in the morning and you're admiring your friend's latest posts.

Ping!

Was that a text on WhatsApp or a message on Facebook?

What are you doing up so late?
Hey sexy how's it going?
Hi!
Can't sleep either huh?
It might even be just a 'wave'.

Do not engage. Do not respond. This is the Horn Dog Hour, and you are not the only woman that is receiving a text or message from this man. A friendly initial chat can soon turn a corner into 'dick pic' land. And that's exactly what they want.

It's a lure, a piece of bait, and they're sitting there waiting for you or some other poor woman to bite. It's just another numbers game. They might be drunk or sober, but the guaranteed truth is they are horny.

Unless it's a family member or a close friend that you trust, don't engage. Every time we do, we encourage them to continue to throw out their lures. Not just to us, but to others too.

If you want to talk to me then text me at a normal hour!

Bread Crumbing

Also known as 'Hansel and Gretelling'.

This is when someone gives you minimum effort but expects maximum return. By this we mean liking your social media posts sporadically whilst sliding into your direct messages occasionally.

They will give you the sense that they are interested in you. However, they have no intention of meeting up with you or getting in a relationship.

These men are just doing this for an ego boost. They will be doing this to hundreds of women daily and weekly.

They will give you just enough attention for you to think that there might be a slight chance of a relationship.

Beware of the serial 'bread crumbers'.

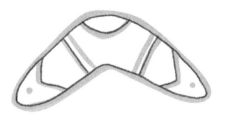

Boomerang

These men can also be known as the Ghosters or Discarders. Usually, they have done something to upset you or treated you badly. You might have blocked them or just gone silent on them. Whatever has happened the air has gone quiet and you will not hear from them for a day, a week or even longer.

But just like a boomerang, they will come back.

Ping!

There's that text.

Hey sexy!

Hey stranger!

How are you?

I miss you...

They'll act like nothing ever happened. They might try and evoke memories and emotions of the past.

Do you remember that time in the Cotswolds?

I've never had the same chemistry with anyone else.

That sex was incredible.

I can't stop thinking about you.

You might hear claims that they are going to get the

help that they need like rehab or counselling. They will tell you that they're in a better place now and they've sorted out their inner demons.

Their words may sound honest, but we find ourselves back at the beginning. It is just an act. They probably even believe their own lies. They might go to one session of therapy, but it won't go any further than that. Sadly during the lockdown the Boomerangs out there will have multiplied. This alongside the Ghosters will confuse many women's heads.

Pick up on it ladies. See them for what they are. Radio silence should prevail.

Girl Friend Story

So a girlfriend met a guy years prior. He was charming, good looking and charismatic. He was everything that she wanted him to be and more. Then the dark veil of truth was lifted. By the end he had lied to her, cheated on her and even physically attacked her. He was an abuser through and through.

One day, years later, he saw her walking along the street which prompted him to DM her. The message said, 'I saw you in town but I was with my son so I couldn't say hello'. The woman didn't reply. He decided to text her again but still the woman didn't reply.

A couple of months later he messaged her again saying he had seen her out walking again. This, of course, was a lie. It was just another attempt to get back into her life again. The man was obviously bored of his current circumstances and saw an opportunity to ruin another woman's life once again.

Boomerangs are never about you. They are about the toxic person being bored and wanting to find a new 'chase' to hunt. If you learn how to see them coming, then you can avoid them. And avoid them you must.

<u>The Projection Section</u>

Projection is another tool that the manipulator has in his arsenal of weapons. If they are cheating on you then they will accuse you of cheating. If they are feeling insecure then they will make you feel the same. They will project whatever thoughts they have onto you as long as it makes them feel better.

You will hear insults as they call you stupid or ugly. They will say you are lazy and have no personality or are unsociable. Deep down they are simply unloading everything that they hate about themselves on you. They would never recognise the fact that they have low self-esteem of course. It is far easier to lower yours.

In order to feel better about themselves they will put others down and make personal and hurtful comments. This in turn also makes them feel more powerful and superior. This can be seen most in those with the infamous God complex. Those on the outside would never believe that they have any doubts about themselves as they project all of their insecurities onto others whilst displaying a solid and proud outer shell.

Projection is once again not about you; it is about their own insecurities. But they will take you down with them. When someone is telling you something about yourself that is hurtful and demeaning, ask yourself this….. Is this about me or you?

HoboSexual

They say that nobody falls in love faster than a man who has nowhere to live. Obviously, this does not apply to all men. But the man who is a manipulator will latch on to someone that has their own home.

They will move extremely fast declaring their undying love and they will push the subject of soulmates (Future Faking). They will get you to sympathise with them about their troubled situation. Whether they are couch surfing or homeless they will press the issue with you and constantly remind you of how they could be on the street.

You will hear tragic stories about their parents and upbringing. They will relay their suicidal thoughts to you in a constant effort to gain your trust and sympathy. They will rely on your empathic tendencies and pluck at your heart strings.

Often the manipulator will not have a reliable job or any job at all. This will lead to you paying all of the bills and risk going into debt for them. It is possible that they have several children from previous relationships where they worked their magic on other women only to abandon them after the thrill of the chase had ceased.

The hobosexual is someone that enters into a relationship to avoid being homeless or being locked down during Covid 19 with their mothers or other family members they are having to co habit with due to their circumstances. Covid 19 would have increased the numbers of hobo sexual men across the globe. You are not their soulmate. You are a means to an end. Watch out for the tell-tale signs of the hobosexual.

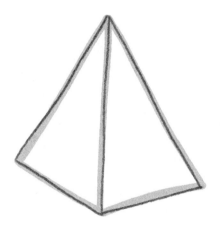

<u>Triangulation</u>

This is where a manipulator will pit people against each other. It could be your friends and you or you against your family. They will use other people as pawns in their game. They might use another woman to make you feel jealous and insecure. It might be to entrap your even further or just for their own amusement.

Triangulation is linked with the attempt to isolate you from your friends and family. If the manipulator succeeds in this, he has got you right where he wants you. Your friends and family will become distant and you will be alone with this man. Watch out for arguments or quarrels instigated by the man. Keep an eye on your friend count. If it starts to decline, then he's getting what he wants.

Poking the Bear

This is usually brought on when the manipulator intentionally creates a situation to invoke negative drama just to see how you react.

It is almost like a drug to them. They need to have drama in their lives. They need to create and control the drama. It is what keeps them alive and they thrive for more. It gives them the energy to keep going. It is their essence for being. Without it they cannot function. And if they can't get it from you, then they will create it elsewhere around you.

You will find this is why many men juggle several women at once. It allows them to create as much drama as possible. You could be the most laid-back person in the world, but they will still prod and poke and criticise everything that you do or say. How you talk, what you wear, how you wear your hair. The prodding comes in all forms from cooking to cleaning to how you do your own job.

They will do this until you explode, and it is likely that you will. But then, you have just given in and fed the beast. You have given him what he wants. Perhaps you have exploded and disengaged from a friendship because he kept telling you certain things about someone you know. One less friend and drama created.

They are always looking for their next hit of the adrenaline rush that they get from controlling situations and provoking negative reactions. Think before you react. Ask yourself why they are telling you something or why they keep commenting on you in a negative way. Don't let them poke the bear and cause you to roar. You will only be giving them the reaction they want.

<u>The Great Escape</u>

If you are lucky enough to recognise when you need to exit stage left from a toxic person and an even more toxic relationship, there are three options available to you.

<u>Block Them</u>

By this we mean cut them out of all social media platforms. This includes Facebook, Instagram, Twitter, Messenger, WhatsApp, emails, texts, calls etc. This also may mean that you need to contact your phone provider to ensure that you are not getting voice mails. You more or less have to remove their ability to contact you on any platform and erase their existence in your life. Don't keep their number written down just in case you one day give in and contact them. Get rid of them and prevent them from contacting you.

Please be mindful that this form of action can ignite a rage from them that you must prepare for. You are now taking control and the abuser/manipulator will be losing control. This is a dangerous stage, and you must be strong and resilient. This is the best thing that you can do for peace, safety and for your own mental health.

However, this could lead to a fall out of epic proportions and there will be consequences with this method.

These people will go to great lengths to rewrite history. To smear your name and tell anyone who will listen how they are the victim and the injured party. You tend to find that these people will migrate to find new friends. They will use any tools available to contact you whilst still trying to destroy you. And remember, there is nothing that the manipulator will not do to make you come back.

Examples of this will be sickness, depression, attempts at suicide or physical injury. They might have suddenly had a car crash or a heart attack scare. There will be a story to lure you back in and it will revolve around them being hurt in some way. They might tell you that they have had a mental break down. They might say that they are thinking of committing suicide or are having suicidal thoughts. They may say that a family member or a close relative is ill or is dying.

The sad truth is that there is no depth they won't sink to in order to get you to contact them again or even meet up. But this is again just part of their game. It's more lies in their fantasy world and they want to drag you back into it.

It is extremely hard to leave a manipulator and it is even harder to leave the relationship when you are co-habiting with that person. It of course gets even more difficult when you are married or there are children involved.

You will need to make a plan and stick to it. Do not leave any paper trails whether it be on the phone or writing anything down. If the manipulator finds out what you are planning to do this could prove very dangerous. The most dangerous time of any abusive relationship is when the 'victim' finally decides to leave. This is when the abuser will risk anything and everything in order to keep you.

It is hard to leave this situation as you have been emotionally and mentally manipulated and although others may say 'just leave' that is easier said than done. You have been trauma bonded with this person and you are likely addicted to the extreme highs and lows of the relationship.

You will feel like your brain has been scrambled. It is similar to weaning yourself off drugs. Sadly, this is all part of the process. Removing a manipulator from your life is like pulling a needle out of your arm and saying, "I don't need you anymore." It takes a long time to get over what you have been through regardless of how long the relationship was.

Girl Friend Story – Block

After going through the process of blocking an ex-partner a friend discovered that a private investigator was following her for over a month. This man would turn up at the local supermarket and even at the local bar where she was drinking at the time. She also had a solicitor contact her with a bill for all of the meals and restaurants that the ex-partner had taken her to in the time that we had dated.

Although strange, these were still all methods for him to contact her and to try to disrupt her life whilst drawing her back into his fantasy world. She kept my barriers up and maintained the block on him.

Another Girl Friend Story

Previously a friend in a toxic relationship had blocked an ex-partner. He then went on to set up several fake Facebook profiles in order to try and stalk her. He then contacted her family and friends and would often call them throughout the night to try and find out where she was.

This led to her friends and family having to block him as well. He even sunk as low and tried to stalk her through their children's social media.

He would turn up at the house and begin to threaten her and shout insults through the letterbox and windows scaring the children in the process.

He alleged that their break-up had caused him to have a mental breakdown. He even faked an illness to try to gain her empathy and attention. He had purposely lost three stone in weight, so that it looked to the outside world that he really was ill. He spread the word to her friends and contacts that she had caused him to have a nervous breakdown. Finally he threatened to move back into the property that they co-owned which prompted her to obtain a non-cohabitation order from the court.

Just another example of the methods these men will use to get what they want or try to get what they had back. Effective blocking can prove very necessary at these times.

Restrict

This is the best option to use when it comes to those particular people that you know are going to cause major problems. For those who have children with the abuser, this is the best option. It enables you to gain some control back over your life. It allows you to set the boundaries and create a level of control which you are setting. Restricting what the other person can do or see from your side of life will strengthen your position. When children are involved this can be the better option to go for without the full-on force of blocking.

But please be aware that this is only likely to be a period of respite, as this person will have their own agenda.

Grey Rock

This is similar to restrict and it should be implemented if you have children or even a shared pet with the abuser. Grey rock is all about becoming very boring and unattractive to the abuser (not in a physical sense). Whenever you are in contact with that person ensure that all messages and phone calls are very bland. Stick to the subject and don't give them any information to work with.

Do not show them any emotion. If they begin to shout or harass you just hang up and end the call. Or if it comes as abuse in a text, just don't reply. Grey rock is vital in demonstrating to the abuser that their words and actions can't hurt you anymore. Give them nothing. Even when they try to push you, and they will, let them see the dullest side of you that you can. Your goal is to remain in contact for only vital subjects, such as children, otherwise offer them nothing else and watch their boredom grow. You want them to get bored so that their contact decreases.

Life Can Be Difficult

Stage managing a relationship with someone that tries to control you is important. To them it is all about the power play. You must learn to decide how someone will treat you and how someone will react or engage with you.

You must decide that sometimes you may have to phase someone on out of your life. This may be a friend, family member or ex-partner. This can come in the form of restricting them through texts and social media.

You may even have to reach out to your own friends and family and ask them to do the same. Believe me, your friends will start to receive the texts from unknown numbers or new friend requests on Facebook. You might get friend requests or followers from fake social media accounts. Viewing your social media stories and accounts.

(Please refer to the section on minions.)

We have even seen emails being sent and letters arriving at family member's households.

If it gets to this point you might have to consider contacting the police especially if this has reached the point of harassment. If it continues or gets really bad you may need to obtain:-

A non-occupation order if you co-own the property together.

A restraining order.

A non-molestation order.

There are many services that specialise in mental, physical and emotional abuse. We will provide more details on how to find and obtain this help at the end of the book.

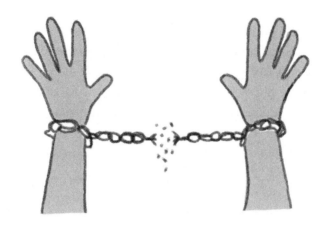

After the Great Escape

It is likely at this point that the abuser will cancel any form of maintenance towards you. They will not be consistent with any payments, clothes for the children or even things like paying for their haircuts. They will also become less consistent and regular with seeing their children.

They will delay paying maintenance or not pay any at all. They will threaten you with solicitors and court action. Even though you know deep down that they do not care at all about them, they will try and gain full custody of the children.

Their main goal now is to make life as uncomfortable for you as possible. Be it through not communicating properly about subjects involving the children, or by just not replying to texts about the house or selling the house and so forth. They will become secretive with their whereabouts whilst still expecting to know yours.

It is likely that they will turn to drink or drink more than they did before whilst blaming you for everything that has happened. They will not accept any form of blame on themselves. In their head, you did this to them, and you are the cause of everything bad. The blame game will begin, and it will continue likely to never end. It is impossible for a narcissist to recognise that their actions have caused or contributed towards the ending of the relationship..

Minions

These are the people that are close to them. They may also be narcissists or just others who have been manipulated by them and fed their sob story of how you wronged them. They will use their minions after the great escape to stalk you on social media on their behalf and to find out information about you. They can be family, friends or even their own children. Whoever they can use to manipulate the situation and gather information.

These minions will help to smear your reputation. They may not be fully aware of what they are doing, or may be content in their role. The manipulator may blackmail the minion to do their bidding for them or the minion may be in awe of the manipulator and are trying to please or impress the toxic person.

They will monitor your actions on social media or

report back if they have seen you talking to another man or even just out of your house. A minion could even be the new or old 'love' interest of the abuser and they believe that you have hurt their partner and therefore must be punished for it. Never underestimate the power the abuser has on other people as well as you.

They get the minions to abuse you and say things on their behalf. They use them to get to you. They use them to make demeaning comments and report on you. They want to see you broken and they want your life to be destroyed. Remember, you left them in ruins, so they want to do the same to you.

If you are a success, be it through your job or personal life, they will not take this well. Watch out for the minions. They may not even know that they are doing it, but they will try to hurt you on behalf of the toxic person. And those who do know what they're doing are far worse.

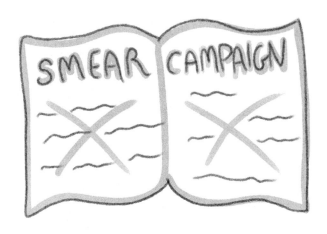

<u>Smear Campaign</u>

Be prepared to find out that the abuser will tell people their own version of events. They will lie and manipulate others to make them believe that you are the narcissist and you have caused all of the problems. Whatever they did to you will be twisted and they will try to make people believe that you did it to them.

And the worrying thing is that they will actually believe their own version of events. They are still living in their own parallel universe where they have done nothing wrong and they are the true victim here. They have created a world for themselves, where people are merely puppets and characters in their story.

Everything they do has a hidden agenda and all the people in their world are pawns in their little game.

The only way to deal with a toxic person in this

situation is to not play the game. Get off the merry go round that you had no idea you were on in the first place. Call it game over and walk away. Let them recruit a new player. Just keep pushing forward and do not look back.

We know that this is hard. We have been there. This is why we wrote this book for you.

Sabotage

A toxic person will go out of their way to sabotage you. It may be to ruin a special day such as your birthday or Mother's Day or any special occasion which means something to you is at risk of being spoiled.

Because it's not all about them.

So they have to make it about them. They will cause an argument the night before the event or they will refuse to attend the event.

They might say that they will turn up to an event and then not turn up at the last minute. They will do these things to cause maximum disruption and emotional upset, especially if there are family members involved.

If they do turn up, it is likely they will cause an atmosphere or an argument. They will relish in ruining your day or humiliating you in front of others. They may whisper nasty comments in your ear, away from others. This might be so that you are the one seen shouting and then they can blame you for causing a scene.

Throughout the relationship you may notice that they will be threatened by your success. They will not support you in future or current endeavours and they will try and knock you down. They do not want you to be success and they do not want you to shine in any way.

If they are worried about your success, they will try and knock your confidence. They will chip away at you, saying comments like you are lazy, you are not ambitious enough, you don't follow through with anything or you never finish anything.

And then they will mention how well that they have done. In their work and their career. How they have achieved all of their goals. They will compare your success to theirs and ridicule you regardless of how well you have done.

If you ever question them on this, then they will say that they are doing this to encourage you to push you further or some other lie about motivation. Please know this is not their intention at all. This is all part of their plan to make you doubt yourself.

This has nothing to do with you. This is all about them. It is deep rooted insecurities in themselves that they are trying to plaster onto you. They are self-saboteurs and will try to destroy you in their process. Destroying good things is all they know how to do, and they will go to any length to destroy you too.

<u>Our Red Flags:</u>

So, what are the day to day tell-tale signs you should be on the lookout for that should get the alarm bells ringing?

For us, these are now deal breakers. AKA Run girl-friend. And don't look back.

..Living with a parent or a friend without a plan for the future.

Hobosexual – tries to move in or starts to move their belongings in to your flat or apartment without asking or discussing it.

Talks about you having a nice place early on in relationship.

..Asking to borrow money for any reason!

Also pay attention to those men who ask you to pay their bills. Phone bills. Car payments. No, never. Not under any circumstances.

Pay close attention to men who expect you to pay to take them out all the time or pay for their meals, clothes or travel.

..Having a Child with them in their social media profile picture, WhatsApp or any visual platform to the outside world.

The reason men or women do this is to create empathy and trust as they want you to think that they are a kind, caring and responsible person.

..Any unexpected and direct messages sent on a social media platform.

These men are using social media like LinkedIn trawling for women. It is a numbers game. They are sending the same message to hundreds of women. And they are just seeing what results and responses they will get. They are preying on women.

..Pay attention to their friendship circle.

Toxic people tend to have sporadic relationships with

friends as it is all about what they can gain from them and what they might need at the time.

If they do have long term friends this will be because the friend keeps them out of loyalty. They will drop in and out of these groups.

You will find that these people are catalysts for drama in any relationship and there are fallouts which they will hide. They will appear and disappear.

They will usually tell anyone who will listen their version of the situation whilst failing to mention their part in any of the events.

..**Strained or no relationship with close family members**. Again they will only give their version of events to justify this.

..**Constantly messaging you on every social media platform, text messages or WhatsApp.** This is also part of the love bombing phase.

They will more or less bombard you with messages throughout the day. Calling you and face timing you at all times (checking up on you). They want to know where you are and who you are with.

..**Having more than one profile or account on social media**.

Having fake social media profiles is not normal behaviour.

.. **Issues about spending money or taking you out**.

Making comments such as let's guess how much the bill is or other such mind games. We are independent women and happy to pay our half.

.. **Lying about their profession or exaggerating their income**.

..**I'm in a hurry.**

They will try and rush you into a relationship, rush you into sex, moving in with you and even encourage pregnancy.

..**Serial Lying**.

They are like the boy who cried wolf. They will tell little white lies all the time. Telling the truth is an anomaly to them. Lying is just what they do. They are professional liars.

Look out for the way that their face changes when they lie. And changes in body language too. Or they may go on the defensive when questioned and stone-wall you with regards to answers, using typically short one-word answers.

..Keeping the relationship secret on social media.
Not making the relationship public.

..Parading the relationship on social media in order to make an ex jealous or for another agenda.

Hearing stories about their ex-girlfriends.
They might tell you that all their ex-girlfriends are crazy, but they were the one with the problem.

..Cheating on their last partner with You.
You will be no different and it will end in the same way, don't be fooled.

..Cheating full stop on any previous partner.

..Isolating you from friends and family.

..Financial Abuse.

This is when they are in control of the finances, so that they have control over you. Control over all credit cards bank accounts which inevitably leads to isolation.

<u>The Aftermath</u>

Life post the toxic person can be very difficult and you will be scarred by the actions, behaviour and even beliefs of the abuser. You may not know right from left and you may be suffering from sleep deprivation and not eating enough or taking care of yourself. You will actually be suffering from a form of post-traumatic stress disorder and your life will be affected more than you would have believed.

The manipulator has spent time warping you and moulding you into what he wanted. This will have contorted the way you think and see things. You will lose trust and faith in people, especially men. Your opinions will have been twisted and may have taken on a slant of the toxic person. You may even sound like them from time to time.

This is completely natural and there is no short-term cure for this grieving process. You must take steps to help yourself through it, be it simply opening up to friends and family or starting therapy. But one way or another you cannot let them win.

<u>Empathic</u>

Sometimes you can be drawn to broken people because you are broken yourself. Or you have empathic qualities where you feel that you can fix or help that person. Or that you are the one person that can break the cycle. For example you believe that you are the woman who can get them to stop cheating on women, gambling or lying.

This will not happen.

You have to work on yourself. Focus on yourself. Focus on your goals. Enjoy your hobbies or find new ones. Build your life the way you want it.

An Empath is someone who has kind qualities and tends to feel that they can fix people. What we have learnt the hard way is that you cannot fix someone other than yourself.

You will sadly end up breaking yourself in the process. You can support someone through a hard time, but you cannot fix them. They can only fix themselves.

And it is down to the empathic person to recognise these traits.

How can you attract a King if you are not acting like a Queen?

You need to be so busy that your King will just fall into your life. If you are still broken, then you are not fully healed from what you are going through. You will attract the same type of person just in a different form.

Focusing on your goals and on your hobbies will help you to stabilise your own life. Shelly started boxing and got into personal training to vent her aggression from the trauma that she had suffered. It enabled her to channel her anger and also it gave her something to get up for.

Louise began taking long walks with her dog as she had lost her passion and zest for life which she was known for.

You do not have to turn to yoga or meditation or turn into a fitness freak. Everyone is different and life progress comes in whatever form or method works for you. It might just be that you take yourself for a walk, starting out small then building up to long hikes. It might be that you watch a funny film and rekindle your passion with the TV.

It might be reading a new book or even writing one. It might be spending time with family or close friends or people who lift you up and make you feel good about yourself. Pay close attention to how you feel when you are around certain people as they can give off energy and vibrations.

Who do you feel happy around and find yourself with more positive energy?

Try new things. Do things that you have never done

before. Maybe with a friend or family member if you do not have the confidence to do them on your own at first. Shelly went to a cardio boxing class with her cousin at the beginning to boost her own confidence. There are plenty of classes out there from exercise, yoga, meditation to cooking, martial arts and more. You might want to learn a new skill and look for an online course at a local college. Have a look at what's out there, you might just find something you fall in love with.

We know that you will be struggling. We know that you will be having sleepless nights and some days will be better that others.

When you first leave a toxic person even just leaving the house is a major milestone in itself.

Shelly remembers when she first moved back into her flat, after spending time at her parent's house, she had no energy to even get out of bed. She would spend days just migrating from the bed to the sofa and back and forth. The highlight of her day was watching Minder on the TV in the afternoon as she was getting up till around 2pm.

But looking back at that point. getting out of bed was something to be celebrated. And you should celebrate every little step of progress that you make in your journey to rebuilding your life. There are no right or wrong rules to overcoming trauma. You have to take each step yourself and ensure that you are on the right path to success. You can do it. Find the help you need in friends, family or therapy. Find the Queen in you and don't ever look back.

Louise and Shelly have a saying:

You are now X amount of days post XX (the toxic person). We would say the person's pseudonym or initials as we would not want to say their name. We wanted the person to disappear and be erased from our lives in every possible way so we would abbreviate their names just like we were abbreviating their impact on our lives.

This wasn't something to entirely focus on but every single day that went by added to the distance we had created from that toxic person. Every day was an achievement just like leaving the flat was a breakthrough.

Sadly, time is the only factor which helps in this situation. But each day is major milestone post that toxic person.

You will suffer from flashbacks and mourning. You will question whether you have done the right thing or not. But one day you will realise that you haven't thought about that person at all.

One day you will feel less anxious.

One day you will feel the memories have faded and you will feel more waves of peace and calm than waves of panic and anxiety.

Shelly started taking CBD oil and drinking tea to help her as well as a natural sleeping aid. As long as it's not detrimental to your health, try anything that calms you down and keeps you calm. One day you will feel this sense of calm and you will once again be in control of your own life and your own path to success.

And you will get to this point. we promise you.

If you are reading this thinking you are not going to get through this. You will!

Louise and Shelly are living proof of two women who have experienced several abusive relationships with men and come out the other side. They have managed to heal themselves and have risen higher than they ever imagined they could.

Louise went to the citizens advise bureaus which helped her get advice and support. This guided her towards what she needed to do during this very difficult period in her life.

Their support ranges from support groups to financial advice with regards to benefits, grants, loans, universal credit and more.

After a few months Louise found that all the emotions she had buried started to flood back in one go like a tidal wave.

Every day in the early days of becoming a single parent, Louise struggled to function. However, she had no choice but to get up and show up as she had three small children and a puppy that were depending on her. Important things such as the school run, putting three meals on the table each day and walking the dog gave her a purpose and with each day it became slightly easier. It also allowed her to see a brighter future with light at the end of the tunnel.

They gave her a reason to get up and to get through each day.

Each day does become easier and shorter. We are not saying that it will not be scary, and it will not be difficult. There were days when Louise cried and then days where she laughed at personal milestones such as moving into a new house with the boys or her children getting good GCSE and college grades.

Louise has a few Tips that she would like to share with the readers of the book.

1. Make sure that you get financial guidance before you leave a toxic relationship.
   We have listed some organisations at the end of this book that you might find useful.
2. Look into getting support for yourself and the children in the form of counselling or groups.
3. Remember to take time out for self care. Run a hot bath, have a facial, read a book or watch a film.
4. Don't be afraid to ask for help and support as and when you need it. You do not have to do everything by yourself. Do not try and take everything on yourself.

Talking openly about her experiences brought everything back and revealed to her just how real it all was. This can become very overwhelming at times.

But Louise found that talking about it really did help. She spoke to family and friends and researched what she had been through using books and the internet. This helped her greatly and allowed her to come to terms with things.

Like the saying goes knowledge is power and Louise and I both truly believe this.

Louise also attended the Freedom project which was run by Women's Aid. She found that it was too raw for her at the time as it brought back lots of memories that had long been buried. But Louise aims to go back one day and complete it.

She saw first-hand how much of a lifeline it was for some women and how important that raw feeling could be for others. Some gained the strength to leave their partners and others went on to gain knowledge and understanding of what had happened to them.

There is no right or wrong answer to who can help you or which organisation is best suited for your situation. The right thing to do, however, is to go looking for help. Once you break that barrier between you and the outside world you have already begun the process of recovery. One organisation may be a better fit for one person than another. Get yourself out there, seek the help that you need and deserve. Never be alone and never allow yourself to believe that you were the one in the wrong.

We would like you do to this short exercise. From Shelly's living your life as a Queen Book

This is a positive affirmation.

Please stand in front of a mirror and say the words below aloud to yourself 5 times.

I am a strong powerful woman.
I deserve to be loved. I am loved by many. I attract money, relationships and friendships easily.
I am a Queen.

Try doing this every morning and make this part of your daily routine.

You might think that this feels strange at first. You might find it hard to look at your reflection and say these words. But give it a go. It can't hurt. Try it right now and say the words out loud.

If you persevere with this exercise you will find meaning and power in the words the more that you say them. Your thoughts will become your words and you will feel the power coming out of your mouth in time.

If you are interested on working on yourself and stepping into your power and reigning your life, then contact Shelly to join her VIP coaching group in 'living life as a Queen'.

You will always carry the scars of your past. But look at them as your battle scars. They are shaping you into the strong woman that you are becoming. The version of you post trauma will be an entirely different person.

You are a survivor.

Everything that you have been through is part of your story and your journey.

Shelly did a lot of work on herself to become the Queen that she is today.

What does it mean to live your live as a Queen?

A Queen feels safe and secure in herself and knows that she can look after herself in all aspects of her being, be it financially, emotionally, physically and spiritually.

She never tries to deprive someone of strength, power or efficiency. She never seeks to weaken someone else for her own gain.

A Queen speaks her mind and knows when she needs to speak up.

A Queen listens to understand, not to be right. She also allows the other party time to speak their mind. Without interrupting.

A Queen is confident and knows her worth. She seeks to empower others while ruling her own life.

If you would like to step into your power, start to reign your own life and live with purpose and confidence, then get in touch with Shelly today.

With this book we are aiming to empower, educate and to give people the tools to escape the toxic person that you were involved with. And like we said, if we have helped one woman and one family, then we have achieved what we set out to do. Which is more than we ever thought we would do.

So this book is for you.

Louise and my vision is that you turn into the Queen that you are. Please share this story with a friend, a cousin, a sister, a daughter, an auntie, a parent or anyone that you know who is in a toxic relationship.

Take back the power that is inside you. We can all be Queens.

There is help out there

Please look at the following websites and agencies that are there to support you. All you have to do is take the first brave step to seeking that support.

www.freedomprogramme.co.uk
The Freedom Programme is for women who want to learn more about the reality of domestic violence and abuse.

www.womensaid.org.uk
Women's aid is a federation working together to provide life-saving services and to combat domestic abuse.

www.refuge.org.uk
A refuge is a safe house where women and children who are experiencing domestic abuse can live and stay free from fear.

www.mindful.org
Meditation is an ancient wellness practise that focuses on training awareness, attention and compassion. In recent years research has found that meditation can reduce stress and anxiety, improve focus and concentration, and increase feelings of calm and relaxation.

www.counselling-directory.org.uk
Counselling is a talking therapy that can help with a

range of mental and emotional problems including stress anxiety and depression.

www.gingerbread.org.uk
The Gingerbread charity is for single parent families. They provide expert advice and practical support for single parent families to live secure happy and fulfilling lives.

www.nhs.uk
The NHS has a comprehensive list of organisations that you can contact when in need of help and support.

www.gov.uk
A **non-molestation order** is typically issued to prohibit an abuser from using or threatening physical violence, intimidating, harassing, pestering or communicating with you. An order could prevent the abuser coming within a certain distance of you, to your home address or even attending your place of work.

A **non-occupation order** is an order which is issued by the family court under part IV of the Family Law Act 1996 and sets out who has the right to stay at the family home, who can return and who should be excluded. An order does not change the financial ownership of a property.

A **restraining order** is a court order which prohibits the abuser from doing certain things such as contacting you or attending your place or work or home address. Breaching (breaking) a restraining order is a criminal offence and can lead to arrest. The court will make the order if the judge believes it is justified and necessary.

Afterword

In Louise's words.

Well you all how we met and how long we have been friends for, but we have so many memories that we've created and shared over the years, especially the most recent.

When the pandemic was announced Shelly ended up having to stay with me, along with my partner at the time.

She was stuck with me my partner, my three teens, a dog and his young daughter coming to stay every other weekend. So as you can imagine, it was a bit of a mad house!

But we gritted our teeth, tried to brush aside our anxieties and set about making some more memories.

We made the most of a very worrying, stressful and uncertain time. We had BBQ's, pool parties for the kids, kitchen parties with games, quiz nights and we went for beach and harbour walks. We also used this time to focus on finishing this book. Sometimes we'd have a few gin and tonics, but we would swear it gave us 'ginspiration'.

We also have a standing joke when it comes to my birthday. I like to do different things each time. We've done Rib Rides (let's just say it didn't end very well), Ghost hunts and scare mazes where we nearly scared ourselves half to death.

She always says, 'one day Lou, you are going to kill me off!'

She's always a good sport and for the love of friendship, she goes along with what I want.

I'm still trying to get her to do 'Tough Mudder', but maybe next year or when Hell finally freezes over Ha ha!

I would also like to thank my boys for being part of my journey and one of the main reasons for co writing this book.

Please know that you three are my biggest achievement in life even if I don't always show it.

In Shelly's Words.

They say that people come into your life for a reason, a season, a lesson or a lifetime.

Well I think I can say that Louise and my friendship is for a lifetime.

And I cannot imagine my life without her. It is nice to have that friend who has been there through growing up, who can remember the people, the stories and the bits you have forgotten

My favourite memories are of her chewing ice cubes during our phone conversations which have been known to go on throughout the night into the early hours of the morning. Dancing on various nights out. There is no one better to dance with than Louise.

We are different, but we know each other inside and out and we always support each other and want the best for one another.

The pandemic brought us close and I will never forget lighting a candle to mark the date that my baby should have been born with Louise during this time.

I feel lucky to have her in my life. And here's to the next chapter of memories for us both.

I would like a moment to thank my Mother and father who raised me, as being adopted was the best thing that has happened to me.

Contact: shelly@fabuliciousfitness.co.uk

The Journey to self-love starts with acceptance and self-love.

To help you take that first step. We have included a few blank lines for you to start your own gratitude Journal.

To start all you need to do is write down each day before you go to bed three things that you are grateful for each day.

These could be things such as

Waking up.

A phone call with a friend.

A relationship with a family member or partner.

Gratitude Journal

....
....
....
....
....
....
....
....
....
....

Printed in Great Britain
by Amazon

34273158R00056